MW01199340

실 비치에 뜬 달
MOON OVER SEAL BEACH

서울문학출판부

MOON OVER SEAL BEACH

실 비치에 뜬 달

YOON SOO PARK
박윤수 한영시집

Translated from the Korean
by Eunhwa Choe
번역: 최은화

Korean Expatriate Literature
California, USA & Seoul, South Korea
&
Cross-Cultural Communications
New York, USA
2017

Copyright ⓒ 2017 by Yoon Soo Park

All rights reserved. No part of this book may be used or reproduced in any manner whatsoever without written permissions, except in the case of brief quotations embodied in critical articles and reviews.

Co-published by Korean Expatriate Literature and Cross-Cultural Communications

First Edition, 2017

Library of Congress Control Number: 2017950625

ISBN 978-0-89304-649-1

First printing of Bilingual Edition: 2017

Korean Bilingual Poetry Series #3

Co-publisher: Korean Expatriate Literature
11533 E. Promenade Dr.
Santa Fe Springs, CA 90670 USA
Tel: (562) 929-2338
E-mail: ychopoet@yahoo.com
www.hewemunhak.com

Co-publisher: Cross-Cultural Communications
239 Wynsum Avenue
Merrick, NY 11566-4725 USA
Tel: (516) 868-5635/Fax: (516) 379-1901
E-mail: cccpoetry@aol.com
www.cross-culturalcommunications.com

Cover design by Mimi Park
Cover art (water color, 8.5 x 4.5" – 2016) by Gianpiero Actis
Printed by: Seoul Munhak Corp.
404 Gongduk-dong, Mapo-gu
Poonglim Vip Suite# 1210
Seoul, South Korea
Tel: 02-070-8711-2638

This book is dedicated to:

My wife of 57 years, who is a wise mother and wonderful wife, our three daughters, who have brought us joy, and our five grandchildren, who have also enriched our lives.

이 작은 책자를 제 가족에게 드립니다.

"현모양처"를 자랑삼은 57년의 동반자 내 아내와 우리들에게 항상 기쁨을 가져다준 세 딸들, 그리고 우리 삶을 풍요롭게 한 다섯 손자들에게 이 작은 책자를 드립니다.

|감사의 글|

　누구보다도 먼저 '시 쓰기'로 내 만년의 갈 길을 인도하여 주
신 분은 조윤호 시인이시다. 그는 '한국 시문학의 세계화'를 위해
현재 한국과 외국의 시인들과의 시 작품 상호교류와 가교 역할
을 하신다.

　나는 Garden Grove의 '글 샘터'에서 조 선생님의 강의를 듣고
시 쓰기에 충동을 받아 그의 끊임없는 격려와 지도 아래 오늘날
까지 시를 쓰게 되었다. 시를 쓰는 동안 90살에 시 쓰기를 시작
한 일본의 노 할머니 '시바다 도요' 시인의 시집 "약해 지지마"를
읽어 얻은 자극과 감동도 내 시인 생활에 큰 동력을 주었다.

　내가 시를 쓰고 먼저 보여 준 사람은 내 아내였다. 아내는 시
인이 아니었지만, 내 사투리 철자법도 고쳐주었고 독자로서 자기
의견을 솔직히 비판할 수 있는 통찰력을 소유하고 있었다. 아내
는 시보다도 산문쓰기를 좋아했고, 드디어 수필로 문예지 "해외
문학" 신인문학상을 받기도 했다.

　미국 뉴욕의 Cross-Cultural Communications 출판사를 통해
출판할 수 있도록 내 시를 영어로 번역해 주신 미국의 전문 번
역가 최은화 씨에게도 감사드린다.

　이 책자 표지를 디자인한 Life 잡지사의 창작 디렉터인 내 둘
째 딸 Mimi에게 감사한다. 영어 교정에는 People 잡지에서 편집
주필로 오랫동안 종사하다가 은퇴한 내 첫째 딸 Jeannie가 수고
를 많이 했다.

ACKNOWLEDGMENTS

Most of all I want to express my sincere thanks to Poet Yoon-Ho Cho, who motivated me to write poetry after I moved to Seal Beach, California, in 2014. He is a world-renowned poet who has made a great contribution by introducing Korean poems to the outside world and by building bridges between poets of Korea and those in other parts of the world. His encouragement and inspiration will remain in my heart forever. During my writing, I was also inspired by Japanese Grandma poetess Toyo Shibata, who started writing poems at the age of 90. I always read her work "Don't Lose Heart" when I get frustrated.

I would like to thank Eunhwa Choe, a Korean-American literary translator, who translated my poems into English for the publication through Cross-Cultural Communications in New York.

I am also grateful to my second daughter Mimi, who designed the cover for this book. She is a Creative Art Director for Life's Special Books. My eldest daughter Jeannie, who was an Executive Editor for *People Magazine*, was instrumental in the English proofreading.

저는 40여 년의 과학교육. 연구와 행정에 얽힌 생활을 해 왔습니다. 그러면서도 항상 마음 한구석에 자연과 인류의 진리를 다른 방법으로 또는 다른 시각에서 추구해보고 싶은 욕망에 가득 차 있었습니다. 인생을 과학적으로 분석 해명하기보다는 우리의 삶의 뜻과 목표를 깊이 이해하고 정립할 수 있는 시간을 마음껏 가져보기를 소망해 왔습니다.

은퇴를 하면서 서운한 감정에 사로잡히면서도 내가 항상 희망하던 것을 할 수 있는 기회가 생길 것 같아서 은퇴생활의 시작을 고대하게 됐습니다. 이제 마음대로 독서를 할 수 있고 글을 쓸 수 있다는 희망에 은퇴의 날을 손꼽아 기다렸습니다.

은퇴를 하고 남쪽 캘리포니아 주 실 비치에 놓여있는 아름다운 은퇴마을 리저 월드에 이사 와서 문예반 모임이 있다는 것을 알게 되어 마음이 흐뭇했습니다.

88년이란 세월이 지나갔지만, 앞으로 다가온 여생을 바라보면서 값있는 삶을 살 수 있도록 노력하고 있습니다. 내가 쓰러질 때까지는 내 인생이 그치지 않고 달려갈 것입니다. Albert Pine은 "내 자신을 위해서 한 것들은 나와 같이 죽어 버리지만, 남을 위해서 또 세계를 위해서 한 일들은 영원히 남고 불멸하다."라고 말했습니다. 이것이 저의 인생철학입니다.

86세 때 처음으로 시를 쓰기 시작했습니다. 처음에는 시상도 잘 안 나오고 실망도 많이 했지만, "약해지지 마"라고 하는 일본의 시바다 도요 할머니의 시를 읽고 분발했습니다. 멋도 모르고 쓰는 시가 줄줄 나왔습니다. 그러다가 시 강의를 듣고 시를 이렇게 써야한다는 것을 알고 나니 시 쓰기가 더 힘들어지고 써놓은 시가 우습기도 했습니다. 시를 쓰는 동안 이런 단계를 거쳐야 하고 "약해 지지마"라는 다짐을 번번이 해야 할 것 같습니다.

일평생 과학과 물리학을 공부한 사람이지만, 시의 세계에 들어오니 내 영혼이 맑아지는 것 같고, 마음의 평화로움을 얻고 어지러운 세상이 모두 다 아름답게 보입니다. 미움도 원망도 없어지고 싫은 사람도 용서할 수 있는 너그러움이 생깁니다. 괴로움과 슬픔도 초월할 수 있게 되는 것 같습니다. 시를 쓰는 동안 내 가슴이 두근거리고 새로운 도전을 할 수 있는 용기를 맛볼 수 있었습니다.

제가 인생의 마지막 길을 달리면서 부족한 시들이지만, 그동안 쓴 것들을 모아 살아온 삶이 아름답고, 행복하였고, 희망과 기쁨에 가득 찼고 값있는 삶을 살아왔다는 사실을 유산으로 가족과 친지에 남기고 싶어 용기를 내고 이렇게 시집을 내어 놓았습니다. 여러분들의 많은 사랑과 편달을 바라고 있습니다.

2017년 7월 15일
로스앤젤레스, 캘리포니아
—박 윤 수

In my 40-year scientific career as a physicist, I always had a burning desire to seek the truth of nature and humanity, not only through scientific methods, but in my heart. I wanted to seek the meaning and objectives of life I was reluctant for my retirement, but on the other hand I was longing for retirement life, since I figured I would have the time and freedom for what I wanted to do besides science. I thought I would have sufficient time for reading and writing as I pleased.

I moved to Leisure World situated in Seal Beach, California. It is a beautiful and peaceful seaside retirement community. There I found many activities, and soon I found the literature class where seniors aspiring to write poems and essays gathered together for learning and composing. 88 years of my life have elapsed; but I am still looking forward to being a valuable and contributing individual for the remainder of my lifetime. Until I falter, I will never cease my activities. As Albert Pine has said, "What we do for ourselves dies with us. What we do for others and the world remains and is immortal." This is my motto of life.

I began writing poems at age of 86. I was frustrated many times. And when I got discouraged I went back to reading "Do Not Lose Heart," by Japanese Grandma poetess Toyo Shibata. Many thoughts of poems floated in my head in the beginning. As I learned more and more about the format of poems and attended the lectures pertaining to how to write the poems, I became reluctant to write the poems. The poems I wrote sounded funny and awkward. I guess one has go through this process to perfect one's poem writing.

I spent all my life studying science and physics, but when I got into the world of poems the world looked different. My mind became peaceful, and the ugliness of the world's reality transformed into beauty. Hatred and remorse disappeared, and I came to forgive many whom I disliked. I was able to overcome sorrow and suffering. My heart was beating when I was writing poems, and I extracted much hope and joy from it. I derived a new challenge and courage from the world of poems.

I have decided to put together my immature poems to show to my friends and offspring that life is full of happiness, hope and joy, and that I have tried to live as a man of value and not as a man of success.

15 July 2017
Los Angeles, California
—Yoon Soo Park

차례
CONTENTS

3. 봄비 SPRING RAIN

4. 별과 달 STAR AND MOON

Part 1

그리움
LONGING

그리움

그대는 겨울을 지나
불어오는 봄바람.

그대가 가까이 있을 때는
보이지 않고
멀리 떨어져 있을 때는
마음에 불을 켜고 살아나는 몸짓.

아침이 되면 늘 찾던
안개 속 관악산 약수터를 돌아
아침 이슬에 푹 젖었던 그대.

고향의 산기슭에서 친구들과 놀던
시냇물은
눈 감으면 대낮처럼 보인다.

LONGING

You are the spring breeze after the long and rough
winter
You were not in sight when you were close to me
When you were away from me
You showed a great gesture alight with lamp in my
mind
I saw you soaked with morning dew
At the Kwan-ak mountain in dense fog
I can see and hear the whispering stream
Even in the bright day time with my eyes closed
I used to play with my childhood friends at the foot
of the mountain
Oh, I miss my hometown dearly
I am longing to return to my old days
and to my dreamland

장미꽃

맑고 고요한 하늘
계절 없이 찾아오는 장미
가시에 찔리면서 가꾸어 주지 않아도
항상 볼 수 있는 장미

봄비 같은 달콤한 향기를 풍겨
아픔도 안겨 주는 가시 같은 장미
불꽃같은 장미를 사랑해서
열심히 가꾸던 장미

사랑하는 이를 위해
부드러운 잎사귀 속에 감추진 장미
밸런타인데이에 그대 가슴에 꽂아 주고 싶었던
장미 한 송이

가시에 찔려 불거진 피가 흐를 때
더 빨개진 한 송이 장미
이제는 가꾸지 않아도 볼 수 있네
사랑하는 이들을 생각게 하는 장미

피어라 또 피어라

ROSES

Clear and serene sky,
Finding roses out of season.
No need top rung risking thorn,
Blooming roses are always there.

Spread a sweet smell like spring rain
Roses with thorns embracing pain,
Loving the roses like flames
Toiled to cultivate.

For loved ones
Roses hidden in soft leaves,
On Valentine's Day I wanted to insert
Them In your heart.
When blood flows punctuated by thorns
Roses add blushing red.

Now no need to cultivate to watch,
Roses remind loved ones that you remember.

Bloom and bloom!

눈 속에서

눈을 뜨니
흰 눈이 소복이 와서
따뜻한 이불같이
온 세상을 덮었네.

길거리의
흩어진 쓰레기
그렇게 시끄럽던
퍼거슨의 폭동도
다 덮어버렸네.

흰 눈이 와서
우리의 얼룩진 가슴도 덮고
미움도 시기도 분노도
덮어주고 녹여다오

따듯한 이불과 같은 눈이
새로운 삶의 기쁨과
희망을 안겨주는
이 감사의 날

IN THE SNOW

When I opened my eyes,
Heaps of snow,
Like a warm blanket
Was covering the whole world.

Scattered trash
On the streets and
Even the uproarious
Ferguson riots,
Are covered.

I wish for the snow
To cover our stained hearts,
To cover the hate, the jealousy, and the anger.

The warm blanket-like snow
Brings new life and joy and hope
In a thankful day.

실 비치에 뜬 달

왜 오늘은 이렇게 달이 보고 싶을까
이전엔 쳐다보지도 않던 달
지금 쳐다보니 아직 구름에 가려있네
종일 뜨거운 햇볕에 시달리던 피곤을
달이 내 근심과 피곤을 풀어주려나

방금 구름을 헤치고 나타난 달
달은 평화와 꿈의 상징이라
아무리 밝아도 쳐다보지도 않던 달
달은 근심도 괴로움도 씻어주는 듯

옛 친구들이 사는 곳에도 비춰주겠지
멀리 두고 온 친구들도 보고 있을까
아무리 밝아도 쳐다보지 않던 달
달은 많은 추억을 가져다준다네.

남쪽바다 실 비치(seal beach)를 찾아와서
마음모아 바라보는 달
달 속에 담긴 많은 전설도 캐어내고
시간 흐르는 줄도 모르고 쳐다보는 달

허공에 매달린 큰달 속에서
꿈과 희망과 기쁨을 찾고
남은 삶의 평온을 찾고자
아무리 밝아도 쳐다보지 않던 달
왜 오늘은 이렇게 보고 싶을까

MOON OVER SEAL BEACH

I'm unsure what prompts my yearning to watch
    tonight's moon,
The same moon I hardly noticed on many nights past,
When I looked up, the moon was draped with clouds,
And my weary body, sun-beaten all day and
Wrestling with worries and fatigue, felt relief.

Just now freshly out of the cloud, appears the moon,
The symbol of peace and dreams,
Which washes off my worries and my pains.

Will this moonlight shine over my dear friends far
    away?
Are my beloved friends watching the same moon
As they reminisce about our shared memories?

I journeyed to this southern seashore of Seal Beach,
And I see the lonely moon pinned up in the sky.
In this big moon I seek my dreams and hopes
    for happiness,
For peace during the rest of my short life.

I'm unsure what prompts my yearning to watch
    tonight's moon,
The same moon I hardly noticed on many nights past.

반짝이는 별들

가슴이 벅찰 때마다
하늘을 쳐다보니
별빛이 깜박거려
옛 우주의 신비를 그려낸다.

어두운 하늘 속에서
반짝거리는 별들아,
소꿉장난하던 옛 친구들을,
어릴 때 뛰어놀던 시내물가를,
모래사장을 비추어다오

반짝거리는 작은 빛 속에서
향수에 사무치는 오늘 이 저녁
작은 불꽃도 강렬한 햇빛보다 밝다

헤어진 친구, 떠나온 고향
오늘도 반짝거리며
매서운 해님이 너를 가릴 때까지
식은 내 가슴을 뜨겁게 해다오

SPARKLING STARS

Each time my heart overflows,
I look at the sky
Starlight blinks
and draws the mystique of old space

Stars sparkling
in this dark sky,
show me
old playmates with whom I played house,
the creek side and sand
where I used to play

This evening overflowing with nostalgia
within the small twinkling light,
small sparks are brighter than strong sunlight

The friend I separated from, the homeland I left
Stars, while you sparkle today,
until the fierce sun covers you,
heat up my cooled heart

새 삶의 시작

은퇴는 새 삶의 시작
용솟음치는 용암과 같이
다시 일어나는 불꽃

빙판을 뚫고 나오는 튤립처럼
새 힘과 희망을 주고
뻗어나는 새 삶의 시작

날개 치며 하늘로 올라가는
독수리같이
새 힘을 얻어

석양과 같이
다채로운 빛깔을
땅 위에 뿌려놓자

값있는 삶을 살 수 있도록
기진맥진할 때까지
내 힘이 감당할 수 있을 때까지
쓰러질 때까지

THE START OF NEW LIFE

Retirement is the beginning of new life,
a spark that rises again
like lava gushing up

Like a tulip that bores through the ice,
the start of a new life stretches out,
the new life that gives new strength and hope

Like the eagle
flapping its wings and climbing the sky,
I gain new strength

Like the sun,
let's sprinkle many colors of light
on the ground

So that I may live a life worthwhile
until I tire
until my strength fails
until I fall

만남

온갖 꽃들 중에
길 위에 구르는 이파리 하나처럼,
희미한 휘파람 소리처럼 다가와
내 인생에 머물며
나를 변화시키는 꽃들

꽃과의 만남은 또 이별에 이어지지만
만남의 기쁨을 안겨주는
꽃들이 아닐까?

꽃처럼 활짝 피었다가
사라지는 만남이 아니라
서로 눈물을 닦아주고
기뻐하며 좋은 친구들이 되는 거야.

AN ENCOUNTER

Among all kinds of flowers
like a leaf that stumbles across the road,
they come as a faint whistle,
remaining in my life,
the flowers transform me.

An encounter with a flower leads to farewell,
still, don't the flowers give the joy
of an encounter?

Not an encounter of a full bloom
that goes away,
but becoming good friends,
who wipe away tears of one another.

파도

높이 솟은
파도가 달려온다.
내 근심을 지우려고

높이 솟은
파도가 달려온다.
내 교만과 미움을 지우려고

파도는 내 마음 같은
바위에 부딪치며 떠나네.
흰 물거품을 남긴 채

근심도 지우고
교만과 미움도 지우고
떠나는 파도.

A WAVE

A high-rising wave
races onward.
To erase my worries

A high-rising wave
races onward.
To erase my arrogance and hatred

The wave crashes
into a rock that is my heart
leaving behind white foam

After
erasing worries and
arrogance and hatred,
the wave leaves.

무지개

끝없이 흐르는
북해의 바다
갑판을 적시는 이슬비
젖은 하늘에 햇살이 빤짝이네.

무지개가 섰다.
하늘과 바다 한 끝에서 저 끝으로
하늘의 다리가.

저 하늘 다리 타고
살금살금 기어 올라가면
신비한 조물주를 만날 수 있으리.
가슴이 뭉클거린다.
내 혼을 흔드는 찬란한 광채.

A RAINBOW

The endlessly flowing
North Sea
a drizzle of misty rain wets the deck
a sunray sparks from the wet sky.

A rainbow arose.
From one end of the sky to the end of the sea,
goes this bridge of the sky.

If I get on the sky bridge
and stealthily climb up,
I could meet the mystical creator.
My heart chokes up.
A brilliant light shakes up my soul.

황혼

붉어지는 먼 서쪽하늘
찬란한 황혼의 빛깔이
흩어진 구름을 장식한다!

금색 홍색 청색의 찬란한 황혼
전원 교향악을 연주하듯이
하나님의 영광을 선포하듯이
하나님의 창조를 찬미하듯이

이제 황혼은
시끄러운 소음을 잠재우고
평온을 가져다주고
안식을 안겨준다

안식 후에는
평화가 오고
지친 삶의 꿈속에서 깨어날 때
새로운 삶의 의욕이 용솟음친다.

TWILIGHT

The crimson tint of the far Western sky
the brilliant colors of the twilight
adorn the scattered clouds!

The golden crimson azure colors of the twilight,
as if performing in full-cast symphony.
To declare the glory of God
To praise the creations of God

Now the twilight
puts the loud noise to sleep,
brings peace
and gives Sabbath

After Sabbath
peace comes
and when awakened from the dream of a weary life
a new motivation of life bubbles.

사랑의 열차

사랑의 열차를 타고
80마일로 달려가네.

그러나 나는 물어보지 않는다.
어느 간이역을 통과하고 있느냐고?

내 인생은
강물같이 고요히 흐르다가
거센 파도같이 분노도 했고
험한 돌바닥을
쏟아지는 눈물로 적시기도 했지.

마지막 남은 사랑의 열차를 타고
한없이 달려가 보고 싶네.
종착역이 그 어디인지는 모르나.

TRAIN OF LOVE

Riding with a speed of 80 mph
on the train of love.

However, I did not ask,
Which stations we are passing.

My life
was like a quietly flowing river,
at times in a fury of wild waves,
over a rough river bed,
drenching it with pouring tears.

On the last train of love
I want to endlessly ride,
not knowing where the last stop may be.

눈 속에 찍힌 발자국

포근한 흰 눈으로 덮여있는
호숫가를 따라서
묵묵히 걷고 있는 아침
햇빛이
눈부시게 반사할 때마다
눈을 깜박거린다.

깜빡거리는 눈알 속에
살아온 인생이 깜박거린다.
푹석푹석 소리 나는 발자국이
찍힐 때마다 내 삶도 찍혀버리는
눈 속에 내 인생의 허물이
찍혀 묻혀버린다.

힘껏 디뎌보자.
지난날의 아픔도 슬픔도 괴로웠던 일도
잘못도 섭섭함도
부드러운 눈 속에 다 묻혀버리도록
호숫가의 흰 눈도
호수의 물과 함께 흘러 내려갈 태니

FOOTPRINTS ON THE SNOW

This morning
I silently followed along
the snuggly white snow-covered lake.
Whenever the sunlight
reflected glared,
my eyes flickered.

In the flickering eyes
life I have lived flickers.
Whenever the crunch of my footprints
imprint, my life imprints as well,
as my exoskeleton
gets buried into the snow.

Let's step on with full force.
The agony, sorrows, tormenting moments,
the faults and the disappointments, too, of the past,
can be all buried into the soft snow,
since the white snow of the lake
too shall flow downward with the lake water.

두 사람

바람이 가는 길을 따라
당신과 함께 여기까지 왔네.

아픔과 번뇌를 다 내려놓고
이제 당신과 걷는
마지막 가는 길.

달빛이 가는 이 길 위에
이제 이 땅의 일로
가슴 아파 할 필요 없이
달빛을 맞으며 두 그림자가 걷고 있으니
얼마나 기쁩니까?

하늘 위에 흘러가는 구름에
이 세상의 모든 것 흘러 보내고
흘러 간 것 다시 돌아오지 않아도
우리가 나눈 사랑만 안고
당신과 걷고 있는 이 길이
얼마나 기쁩니까?

TWO PEOPLE

Following the path of a wind
I came all the way here with you.

Unburdened of all pain and anguish
you and I on
the last road together.

On this road where the moonlight goes
and on this land no longer
with painful heartaches
under the stream of moonlight two shadows walk
how joyful is this?

Onto the cloud floating in the sky
let us float all worldly things
even if those that floated away never come back
only with the love we shared
on this road where I walk with you
how joyful is this?

Part 2

파피꽃
POPPY BLOSSOM

해 뜨는 지평선

멀리 바닷물 건너
하늘과 바다를 갈라놓은 지평선
붉은 태양빛이 흘러나온다.

누가 하늘과 바다를 갈라놓았나?
그 사이에서 나오는 햇빛이
유난히 아름답구나.

오늘도 기쁨을 가져다줄까?
웃음과 행복을 뿌려놓을까?
슬픔과 눈물이 없는 하루.

풍요로운 인생살이
서로 나누며 돕는 사랑
서광의 아침이여.

SUNRISE ON THE HORIZON

Across the far ocean
from the horizon that separates the sky from the
ocean
flows out the crimson light of the sun.

Who separated the sky from the ocean?
The sunlight that seeps from the between
is spectacularly beautiful.

Would it bring forth joy today as well?
Would it spread laughter and happiness?
A day of no sorrows and tears.

A productive life
A love of sharing and aiding
A new light of the morning.

기다리는 봄

3월이 되면 봄의 교향악으로
시끄러웠는데
사철이 없는 남가주에서는
나비도 벌도 볼 수 없어

꽃봉오리도
새싹도 볼 수 없어
이렇게 변함없는
인생살이 편하기는 하구나.

싸늘했던 겨울바람이
갑자기 뜨거워져
아, 이제 봄이 오는가보다 느끼기는 하지만
마음이라도 가다듬고

새 친구 이웃이나 찾아보자.
기다리는 봄이 서둘러 올 때까지
고독도 외로움도 벗으로 삼고
봄을 기다려 볼까.

WAITING FOR SPRING

When March came it was noisy
with the symphony of spring.
In the southern California, without four seasons,
butterflies and bees are no where to be seen.

No flower buds
No new leaves
In this never-changing way,
life is easy.

When the cool winter breeze
suddenly becomes hot,
ah, the spring finally will be here, one feels.
I pull myself together.

Let me seek out new friends and neighbors.
Until the waiting spring hurriedly comes,
with dismal solitude and loneliness,
shall I wait for the spring.

나비같이 날개를 달고

바람도 없는데 노란 꽃송이가 날아간다.
두 날개를 폈다 접었다
눈부신 햇빛이 타는 창공으로
훨훨 날아간다.

같은 꽃을 찾아주고 또 찾아준다.
나도 나비같이
찾고 또 찾는 고향이 있고
나비가 될 수 있다면

먼 산, 먼 바다
세상을 훨훨 날아다니며
꽃에서 꽃으로
행복을 찾고 싶어.

AFTER DONNING BUTTERFLY WINGS

Even without a breeze, a yellow blossom flies away.
Folding and unfolding its two wings,
towards the dazzling sunlight-filled sky,
it flutteringly flies.

Seeking out the same flower again and again.
I, too, like a butterfly
have a hometown to seek out again and again,
if only I could become a butterfly.

To faraway mountain, faraway sea
flutteringly fly over the world
from a flower to a flower
in search of happiness.

저녁노을

붉은 황혼이 물들었다.
햇빛으로 물든 장대한
황혼의 빛깔
구름의 찬란한 색깔을 보여주는
저녁노을.

금색 홍색 구름으로 조립된
전원 같은 저녁노을,
전원 교향악이 울려 나올 듯

오늘도
하늘이 당신의 영광을 선포하는 저녁노을
인생의 황혼도 이렇게 축복하리라.

우리 다같이
기뻐하고 감사하는 황혼
황혼은 아름답다.

SUNSET GLOW

The twilight is dyed in crimson.
The sunlight drenches the mighty
colors of twilight.
The sunset glow
showcases the brilliant colors of the cloud.

The sunset glow looks like
a countryside gathered in gold red clouds,
as if a full symphony of music would spread.

Today
the sky proclaims your glory through the sunset glow.
The twilight of life will be blessed this way, too.

Let us all
be joyful and grateful for the twilight.
The twilight is beautiful.

4월

겨울은 가고
봄바람과 같이
기쁨과 희망을 싣고
사랑의 새싹을
몰래 심어다주는
4월이 왔습니다.

굳어진 마음도
녹아나고
파란 가슴으로
싹이 트네요.
시기와 증오도 다
달아났습니다.

헌것은 묻어버리고
새것을 가져다주는 4월
죽었던 사랑의 불꽃이
살아나는 사랑의 달.

APRIL

The winter has gone
and April
that stealthily sprouts
the seedling of love
with the spring wind
with joy and hope has come.
Even the hardened heart
has thawed out
sprouting
with a green breast.
The envy and loathing
have run away.
Burying the old
April brings the new,
and the flame of love comes
back to life in this month of love.

부활의 기쁨

새벽을 알리는
밤하늘의 별들은
부활을 노래하며

전쟁과 살인이 가득한 이 땅에
미움과 불신의 한가운데에
부활의 기쁜 소식이 찾아왔네.

십자가의 사랑도 잊은 듯이
분노와 시기가 가득한 우리 마음속에
부활의 아침은 고요히 찾아와

희망과 소망과 기쁨을 가득 싣고
참된 자유와 평화의 길이 된
부활의 기쁨을 버릴 수가 없지.

JOY OF RESURRECTION

Signaling the dawn
the stars of the night sky
sing of the Resurrection

In this land full of wars and murders
amongst hatred and distrust
the good news of Resurrection came.

As if forgotten of the love of the Cross
to our hearts full of fury and envy
the morning of Resurrection silently came

fully loaded with hope, wish, and joy
the road of genuine freedom and peace
the joy of Resurrection cannot be abandoned.

봄바람

갑자기 싸늘한 바람이 지나간다.
스치는 찬 바다바람이
내 영혼을 잠 깨운다.

겨울이 미련이 있어
봄을 쫓아
떠나지 못 하고 달려왔지.

마치 천둥처럼 찾아온 바람
봄을 시기해서
나뭇가지 사이로 스치며 지나가

오늘도 기다리던 봄은 찾아왔지만
찬 바다바람은
새싹을 마구 흔든다.

SPRING BREEZE

Suddenly a frosty breeze passes by.
The grazing cold sea breeze
wakes up my slumbering spirit.

The winter with lingering attachment
would not leave behind the spring
so it comes back running.

The breeze that came back like thunder
envious of the spring
weaves through the tree branches.

Even though a long-awaited spring is here
the cold sea breeze
shakes up the new sprouts.

파피꽃

미의 여왕
봄의 주인공처럼
화려하게 겹친 꽃
눈부신 햇빛 속
봄바람에 살랑이네.

꽃봉오리 주렁주렁
시녀처럼 둘러싸고
지나는 사람마다
걸음을 멈추고
정들게 바라보네.

찬란한 모습
영화도 아름다움도
소멸되고 말 테니
봄바람에 사라질 때까지
마음껏 즐기려네.

POPPY BLOSSOM

The queen of beauty
as a lead of spring
the splendidly petal-layered flower
under the brilliant sunlight
gently sways with the spring wind.

The flower buds cluster around
like ladies-in-waiting
and the passersby
stop and
affectionately gaze at them.

The splendid image
in due time the splendor and beauty
will extinguish
before it disappears with the spring wind.
enjoying it fully till then.

나눔의 사랑

산다는 것은
슬플 때도 있고
기쁠 때도 있지.

괴로움과 슬픔이 가슴을 저리게 해도
사랑은 아픔을 견디게 하는 거야.
무지개처럼

오늘도 사랑과 기쁨으로
하루의 문이 열리고
하루의 문이 닫히는 인생길.

나누어 사는 인생
얼마나 기쁘고 행복한가.
정을 나누고 재물을 나눌 수 있다는 것
내 이웃의 불행을 행복으로 만들 수 있는 인생

나눔의 사랑은
봄바람처럼 기쁨과 웃음을 싣고
우리 속에 들어오네.

행복을 나누어
동행하며 사는 인생길
인생은 기쁘고 아름다운 거야.

THE LOVE OF SHARING

In living
there are moments of sorrow
and moments of joy.

When the heart aches with sufferings and sorrow
love lets one withstand the pain.
Like a rainbow
love and joy
open the door to today
and close the day in the road of life.

The life lived in sharing
—how joyful and happy!
That affection and riches can be shared.
That life can turn my neighbor's unhappiness
into happiness.

Love of sharing
carries joy and laughter like the spring breeze
and penetrates within ourselves.

Sharing happiness
accompanying the road of life
life is joyful and beautiful.

아침

아침은 희망
하루의 시작
돛대를 달고 떠나는 어선같이
희망을 신고 달리는 시작
기쁨을 가져다주는 이 아침

잠에서 깨어나지 못한 얼굴로
아침 하늘을 쳐다보지 말아야 해.
지난날의 어두운 마음으로
아침을 마지하지 말아야 해.

새로운 아침 입김을
하늘 높이 뿌려보자.
기쁨을 가져다주는 이 아침.

MORNING

A morning is a hope
A beginning of a day
Like a fishing boat departing with a sail high
it's the beginning of a run with hope
This morning brings us the joy

One must not look up to the morning sky
with a face still not awake
One must not greet the morning
with the dark heart of the past day

Let us spread the new morning breath
high up into the sky
This morning brings us joy

서울의 5월

아무리 세월이 흘렀어도
서울의 5월은
젊음의 상징
푸른 물 냄새가 코를 찌른다.

짙은 녹색으로 묻혀버린 산기슭
진달래와 개나리는
어딘가로 살아졌지만
문득 다가온 한 뭉치의 희망.

희망의 불꽃으로
타고 있는 서울,
탁한 공기도 휘덮고
약동하는 생명.

영혼을 사로잡은
내 고향 서울의 모습
무성한 힘의 상징
요동하는 5월의 모습이 보인다.

MAY IN SEOUL

Even with many years past
May in Seoul
is a symbol of youth
The green smell of water stings the nose.

The mountain shoulder enveloped in rich green
azaleas and forsythias
have faded to the unknown
but a bundle of hope suddenly appears.

Seoul burns
with flame of hope,
enclosing the stuffy air
and thrives with life.

Captivating the soul
my hometown the image of Seoul
The symbol of full energy
The pitching and rolling image of May.

자연의 신비

가슴이 요동친다.
이것이 하나님의 경륜인가.
그랜드 캐년 노스림의 장관.

강물이 갈라지고
절벽이 우뚝 솟은
우주의 드라마
내 잠든 영혼을 뒤흔든다.

그림 같은 지층
창조주의 섬세한 작품
역사의 수레바퀴 속의
한 점 같은 인간.

THE MYSTERY OF NATURE

The heart beats in thunder.
Is this God's experience and knowledge?
The grand view of the Grand Canyon North Rim.

The river divides
the cliffs stand tall
the drama of the universe
shakes my sleeping spirit.

The picturesque geological strata
A delicately detailed artwork of the Creator
In the wheel of history
a dot is a human.

그대의 손

그대의 부드러운 손을
내가 잡고 있을 때
달빛 속에 있는 듯이
그날의 그리움이 살아난다.

지난 세월 속에
쭈굴쭈굴 굳어버린 그대의 손을
지금 내가 꼭 잡고 있어도
달빛은 더 밝아온다.
애처로운 마음에

YOUR HAND

When I hold
your soft hand
as if it's within the moonlight
my yearning from that day rises.

In the passing of time
your wrinkly hardened hand
even as I hold tightly
the moonlight becomes brighter
with sorrowful heart.

Part 3

봄비
SPRING RAIN

봄비

봄비가 보슬보슬
말없이 찾아오는 친구같이
반갑고 기쁘다.
기다리던 단비,
뛰어나가 얼굴을 든다.

푸른 나뭇잎
파란 광채를 띠고
내 얼굴 적시는
빗방울도
부드럽다.

비속에 젖은
꽃들 속에
구겨진 내 마음도 고뇌도
묻어버리는
봄비.

SPRING RAIN

The soft drizzle of spring rain
like a friend who visits without a word
pleasantly and happily welcomed.
A long-awaited sweet rain,
I run out and tilt my face up.

Green tree leaves
blue sparkle-tinted
raindrops
ever softly
wet my face.

Amongst the rain-soaked
flowers
my crumpled heart and anguish
are buried by
spring rain.

신라의 흔적

역사의 한가운데서
헤매는 이 밤
영광도 명성도 사라지고
무너져 버렸지만
역사의 유적은
아직도 남아있네.

궁정의 권력도 영화도
땅 속에 묻힌 신라의 고적,
찬란했던 문화의 유산 속에서
헤매는 이 밤
안압지에 서 있는 궁정. 불국사
현대 문명의 위력 속에서도

우뚝 서 있는 신라의 자랑들
선비와 화가와 도자기공
그들의 땀과 눈물로
빚어낸 문화의 산물들
흥금을 울리게 하는
신라의 산물에 감탄하는 이 밤.

우리도 역사의 유산이 돼서
후세의 자손들이
찾아주는 역사의 밑둥치가 되어야지.

TRACE OF SILLA

In the epicenter of history
wandering on this night
the glory and fame have faded
fallen and abandoned,
but the ruins of history
still remain.

The imperial court's power and splendor
are buried under the ruins of Silla.
Amidst the brilliant cultural inheritance
wandering on this night,
the imperial court stands in the Anapji Pond.
Bulguksa Temple.
Even under the force of modern civilization,

Silla's success towers proudly.
Scholars and artists and potters
and their sweat and tears
produced cultural artifacts
that touch the heart
and in awe by them on this night.

We, too, should become the inheritance of history
as the solid root for
future generations to visit.

작별

이제는 떠납니다, 친구들이여!
너무 슬퍼하지 맙시다.
또 만날 테니까.

짧은 시간이었습니다.
만났던 즐거움을
껴안고 가겠습니다.

기쁨도 그리움도
눈물에 씻겨 내리지 않게
많은 눈물을 흘리지 않겠습니다.

정든 고국의 산촌
고향의 때 묻은 옷을 입고
떠납니다.

그러나
미련 없이 떠납니다.
또 만날 테니까.

FAREWELL

I am leaving now, friends!
Let's not be too sad,
since we shall meet again.

It was a short period of time.
I will go on embracing
the joy of having met.

So the joy and the longing
won't be washed away by tears,
I will not cry many tears.

Donning my beloved homeland's
mountain dirt-tinged cloth-
I am leaving.

However
I leave without regrets,
since we shall meet again.

모하비 사막

이웃을 위해
봉사하려고 내 온 힘과 정성을
퍼부었습니다.

값있게 진실 되게 산다는 것이
그렇게 쉬운 일이 아니었습니다.
모하비 사막처럼 매서운 비난과 비웃음에
비틀거리고 흔들리기도 했지만

험한 풍란에 부딪쳐
한숨도 많이 짓고 낙심도 했고
육신의 피곤함도
많이 느끼기도 했습니다.

어려움과 고달픔 속에서
기쁨을 찾고
불타는 가슴 속에서
성취의 광명을 바라보며

기울어지는 남은 인생도
아름다운 노을처럼
빛을 비치며
참되고 값있는 삶을 살아야지

MOJAVE DESERT

To help others
I volunteered and poured
all my strength and dedication.

It wasn't easy to live
a life of worth and truthfulness.
I have stumbled and wavered under
the harsh, like Mojave Desert, criticisms and ridicules

confronted with perilous storms
sighed many sighs and despaired too
and felt worn out
from physical weariness.

From hardships and exhaustion
I have found joy and
from the passionate heart
I have looked upon the bright light of accomplishments

and with the rest of declining life
like a beautiful sunset
I will shine the light
and live life with truthfulness and worth.

그늘

앞마당의 고목
나도 저렇게 자라
커다란 그늘이 되고 싶네.

노인 마을의 이웃들에게
쉼터가 되는
커다란 그늘.

"아메리칸 드림"을 품고
바다를 건너온 젊은이에게
커다란 그늘이 되고 싶네.

흩어져 있는 옛 친구들
한자리에 모여 즐길 수 있는
커다란 그늘.

SHADE

An old tree in the front yard
I want to grow like it and
be a wide shade.

To the neighbors in the senior village
for a resting place under
the wide shade.

For the young person with American Dreams
who came across the Ocean
to be a wide shade.

To the scattered old friends
who would enjoy gathering under
the wide shade.

발자국

모래밭을 걸으니
4개의 발자국이 따라온다.

눈 속을 걸어도
따라오는 발자국
힘 있게 밟으면
더 뚜렷한 발자국.

길을 잃을까 봐
나를 따라 올까?
항상 나를 지켜주는 그 발자국.

나를 지켜 주는
동반자같이
따라오는 4개의 발자국.

FOOTSTEPS

When I walk on the sand
four footsteps follow me.

The footsteps follow
the walk on the snow.
The footsteps become sharper
when stepping with strength.

Are they following me
afraid of getting lost?
Always protective footsteps.

They protect me
companion-like
the tagging four footsteps.

그림자

나와 그림자
보름밤에 걸어가는 너와 나
영원한 동반자
오른쪽으로 가면 너도 오른쪽
왼쪽으로 달리면 너도 왼쪽

내가 달리면 숨차게 달려오고
갑자기 멈추면 말없이 멈추는
영원한 동반자
고독한 밤도
나와 같이 하는

떼어놓고 싶어도 떨어지지 않는
내가 울면 같이 울어주는
충직한 동반자
항상 나를 따라오는
유일한 벗

SHADOW

I and the shadow
You and I walking under the full moon
Forever companions
When I turn right you turn right too
When I turn left you turn left too

When I run you breathlessly run too
When I stop suddenly you stop silently
Forever companion
Even on the night of solitude
I am with you

Even if I want to pull off you won't come off
When I cry you cry along with me
A loyal companion
Always following me
My one and only friend

나눔의 기쁨

나눈다는 것
사랑도 나누면 기쁘고
재물도 정도 나누면
기쁨도 더 커지는 것

기쁨이 행복도 낳고
이웃을 행복하게 해 준다면
삶에 활기가 생기고
기쁨도 더 커지는 것

나눔의 기쁨은
굴러가는 눈뭉치
커지고 커져서
보람 있는 기쁨의 꽃을 피우리.

JOY OF SHARING

The act of sharing
When one shares love it brings joy and
when the riches and the affections are shared
the joy becomes larger

Joy begets happiness
when one brings happiness to a neighbor
living is energized and
the joy becomes larger

The joy of sharing
is a rolling snowball
becoming larger and larger
blossoming into fruitful joy.

소나기

하늘 구멍을 뚫고
쏟아지는 소낙비
나뭇잎을 흔들고
먼지를 흘러내려
더 푸른 나뭇잎.

푸른 잎을 보고
기뻐하는 소나기
먼지를 닦아주는
행복한 소나기
나도 소나기처럼
먼지를 닦아주며 살아가리.

도와주는 행복
잠자는 영혼을 깨워주는
소나기
평화와 희망을
되살리고
슬픈 눈물도 씻어주리

RAIN SHOWER

With a drilled hole in the sky
shower of rain pours
shaking the tree leaves
washing away the dust
bringing greener tree leaves.

The rain shower is joyful
seeing the green leaves
rinsing off the dust.
The rain shower is happy.
I, too, shall be like the rain shower
spending life washing away dust from others.

The happiness of helping others
awakening sleepy soul
the rain shower
bringing back to life
the peace and the hope
washing away the sorrowful tears, too.

이화의 여인들
-약대 동문의 부군

내 집에
아름다운 배꽃 한 송이
피었다.

볼수록 너무 아름답고
귀여워
아침저녁으로 바라본다.

이렇게 배꽃을 좋아하다 보니
점점
이화의 여인들도 사랑하게 되었다.

WOMEN OF EWHA

Husband of Ewha Womans University College of Pharmacy Alumna

In my house
a beautiful pear blossom
bloomed.

Prettier by the sight
and adorable
I gaze at it morning and night.

As I like the pear blossom
more and more
I have come to love the Women of Ewha, too.

한 송이 꽃

모든 꽃이 다 져버려도
당신은 끝까지 남아있는
한 송이 장미.

짙은 안개가 휘덮고 있는
오늘 아침도
당신 웃음 때문에
세상을 뚜렷이 내다 볼 수 있네요.

때로는 흔들리는 사랑
사랑도 흔들리며 피는 꽃같이
굳게 뿌리박으며 줄기를 세우지.

당신이 곁에 있기에
삶의 기쁨이 넘치는
이 인생길.

ONE BLOSSOM

Even when all the flowers wither
you are the remaining
one rose blossom.

Even on thickly fog-covered
morning like today
because of your smile
I could see the world clearly.

At times our love wavers
love, too, like waveringly blooming flowers
should root deeply growing the stem.

Because you are next to me
living overflows with joy
on this road of life.

코스모스

앞뜰을 지나갈 때마다
반겨주는 코스모스
가냘픈 그 모습 볼 때마다
꼭 안아 주고 싶어.

차가운 가을바람에 스칠 때면
흔들리는 그 모습이 애처로워
꼭 붙잡아 주고 싶어
가냘픈 그의 아름다운 모습.

오늘도 찬바람 속에서
흔들거리는 그대는
분홍색 자주 색깔의 미소를 띠우며
나를 부를 듯이 흔들거리니

그대를 바라보면,
고개 숙인 그대 앞에 서면
수줍어 지는 내 마음
내 얼굴이 붉어진다!

COSMOS

Whenever I pass the front yard
cosmos flowers greet me.
Whenever I see its frail form
I want to give it a firm hug.

When the chilly autumn wind grazes
the wavering stems look so pitiful.
I want to hold on to it tightly
the delicately frail pretty form.

In today's cold wind
you are swaying
with pink maroon-hued smile
swaying as if to call me.

When I look upon you,
when I stand before your bowed head
my heart becomes bashful
my face becomes crimson!

지나간 세월

파란 잎사귀에 피어난
백합 같은 흰 얼굴이 있어
나는 맹세했지.
기쁠 때나 아플 때나 슬플 때나
아니, 죽음이 우리를 떼어놓을 때까지
서로 위하고 사랑한 세월
꿈같이 흘러갔네.

그 작고 가냘픈 몸이지만
쌀가마니를 들 힘이 나왔고
정원을 가꾼다고 계곡을 찾아다니며
예쁜 돌멩이를 줍던 그대.
이제는 기력도 쇠퇴한 듯
발걸음도 비틀거리다니.

지나가는 사람들이
예쁜 아가씨 보라고 소곤거리던
그대의 흰 얼굴도
세월의 가혹한 장난을 이기지 못하고
까만 점들이 많이 생겼구나!

THE PASSED TIME

Before a face fair as a lily,
blooming among the green leaves,
I vowed:
In happiness, in sickness, in sadness,
no, until death do us apart.
The times we cared and loved
have passed like a dream.

With a small and frail body,
a strength to lift a large rice bag emerged,
and you searched valleys picking up
pretty rocks to adorn the garden.
Now that vigor has declined
and the steps waver.

The people passing by
used to whisper how pretty,
but even your fair complexion
couldn't beat out time's cruel mischief
dotted with dark spots!

Part 4

별과 달
STAR AND MOON

가을이 오면

가을이 오면
설레는 이 마음
이제 다 내려놓고

겸손하게
떨어지는 잎사귀처럼
붉은 열매같이

탐내던 밤송이도
유혹하던 붉은 감도
위에서 아래로

자랑도 교만도 내려놓고
받은 은총과 사랑을
아래로 건네야 할 이 가을.

WHEN THE AUTUMN COMES

When the autumn comes
I shall let down
my fluttering heart

in modesty
like the shedding leaf
like the red fruit

the coveted chestnut too
the luring red persimmon too
from top to bottom

should let down boastfulness and arrogance.
The endowed blessings and love
should be given this coming autumn.

한군데 모여서

1년 동안 헤어졌던 가족이
한자리에 오순도순
보고 싶었던 자식들

전화 오기만 기다리던
사랑하는 핏줄들
그것이 무엇이기에
그렇게도 보고 싶을까?

큰 손녀가 태어났을 때
그 아이가 대학교 갈 때까지 살아있을까 했더니
내년에는 대학을 마친다고
이제는 시집가는 날을 보고 가야지.

할아버지 할머니하고 달려오면
동전 다 털어서 잡비 쓰라고 주었는데
지금은 다 어른이 됐구나.

세월은 화살같이 날아가네.
실컷 사랑하자.
사랑은 줘도 줘도 끝이 없네.

GATHERED IN ONE PLACE

The family after one year of not seeing
harmoniously gathered in one place
the children we longed to see.

Just waiting for calls from
beloved blood-relations.
What is it about it that
we so achingly long to see?

When the oldest grand-daughter was born
I wondered whether I'd be around to see her go to
college
next year she will be done with college
now I must witness her wedding day before I depart.

When she came running Grandpa! Grandma!
we used to give her last of our coins for her sundry
expenses
now she's almost an adult.

Time flies like an arrow.
Let's love to our heart's content.
Giving love is done without an end.

감사

오늘도 잔잔한 호수에
스치는 바람을 느낄 수 있으니
높은 하늘, 넓은 들, 깊은 산
오늘도 볼 수 있으니
감사한 일 아닌가?

이웃을 사랑하고
배울 수 있다는 것
남을 위해서 뭔가를
할 수 있다는 것
얼마나 감사한 일인가?

가족과 같이 한자리에 모여
감사절을 지낼 수 있다는 것
아직도 동반자가 있어
나를 챙겨주니
얼마나 감사한가?

감사한 마음은
반드시 얻은 후에만 있는 것이 아니고
잃었을 때도 있는 것
감사하는 마음은
항상 있기 때문에

GRATITUDE

That I could feel the breeze
passing over the calm surface of the lake
and that I could see
the high sky, vast prairies, deep mountains,
aren't these thankful things?

That I could love my neighbor
and learn,
that I could do something
for others,
aren't these very thankful things?

That I could be among my family
spending the Thanksgiving Day
and that I still have my companion
who looks after me,
aren't these very thankful things?

The heart of gratitude
is not only there when received
but still there when lost,
because the heart of gratitude
is always there.

여신상의 눈물

잔잔한 허드슨 강물이
심히 요동을 치고 있다.
강을 휘덮고 있는 안개도
유난히 짙은 아침.

안개 속으로
어렴풋이 보이는
자유의 여신상의
슬픈 모습.

오늘도 테러가 일어났다.
끊임없는 폭행에 분노하였는가,
짙은 안개가 여신의 눈물 때문인가,
유난히 철렁거리는 허드슨 강물도

격분한 파도를 잔잔케 하자.
여신의 눈물을 닦아주자.
폭력은 가라!
평화의 신이여 자유의 신이여.

TEARS OF THE STATUE OF LIBERTY

The tranquil Hudson River
fiercely undulates.
The fog that's covering the river
is especially thick this morning.

Through the fog
the sad apparition
of the Statue of Liberty
can be hazily seen.

A terror happened yet again today.
Is the fury from the endless violence,
in the thick fog tears of the Statue of Liberty,
and the extreme undulation of the Hudson River, too?

Let us calm the enraged waves.
Let us wipe the tears of the Statue of Liberty.
Be gone, violence!
The Goddess of Peace The Goddess of Liberty.

다시 찾아오는 봄

살금살금 걸어오는
당신의 발자취같이
봄의 소리가
귓속에 스며드네요.

그렇게 기다리던 봄
이제 오면
오염된 지구를
바로잡아 다오.

전쟁과 살인에 가득한
피 묻은 이 땅을
진달래꽃으로
빨갛게 물들여 다오

요동치는 이 땅 이 물결
그대가 와서
추함 없는
평온을 가져다 다오

SPRING COMES AGAIN

Walking stealthily, stealthily
like your soft steps
the sound of spring
seeps into my ears.

When the long-awaited spring
finally comes
let it right
the polluted earth.

On this bloody land
filled with wars and murders
dye it crimson
with azalea blooms.

Let spring come
to the roar of this land this water
and bring tranquility
without the ugliness.

합창단

황혼의 행복을 누리려고
모여든 노인마을
새들 같은 노인들
노래 소리가 요란스럽게
온 마을에 울려 퍼진다.

지나온 삶의 상징인 듯
우렁차고 힘센 목소리
가슴이 뭉클하다.
감사와 기쁨에 얽힌 찬양소리
온 마을을 뒤 흔든다.

쩍쩍거리는 새들같이
하나님의 경륜을 찬양하며
주신 삶과 재능을 감사하는
영광을 올리는 합창단
봄의 교향악을 이룬다.

THE CHOIR

To enjoy the happiness of twilight years
gathered at the senior village
the birdlike seniors
singing songs boisterously
spread all over the village.

As if symbolizing the lives lived
the voices are rich and full with strength
choking up the hearts.
The praise of gratitude and happiness
rocks the whole village.

Like twittering birds
praising God's experience and knowledge
being thankful for life and talent,
the choir raises the glory high
creating a spring symphony.

고독

참새 한 마리가
창문 밖 나뭇가지에
홀로 앉아
석양 하늘을 물끄러미 쳐다보고 있네.

저 새처럼
홀로 있는 시간
쓸쓸하지만
내 영혼을 속속들이 들여다 볼 수 있는 시간
고독은 마치 거울 속에 비치는 나같이

삶의 깊이를
돌이켜 볼 수 있는 시간
지나간 일 옛 친구들
내 마음속 구석구석을
뒤집어 볼 수 있는

지쳤던 내 마음이
높은 하늘과 같이 맑아지고
깊은 호수같이
맑아지고 아름다워지네.

SOLITUDE

A lone sparrow
sitting alone
on the tree branch by the window
gazes at the sun-setting sky.

Like that bird
the time of solitude,
although lonely,
is the time to thoroughly check on my soul
as solitude is like looking at my own reflection
in the mirror.

The time of introspection
looking back at the depth of life
the past events, old friends
every nook and corner of my heart
turned inside out and observed

My tired soul
becomes clear like the high sky
clear and beautiful
like a deep lake.

별과 달

공중에 나란히 매달린
별과 달

다정한 부부같이
내가 달일까? 별일까?
나는 둥글고 큰 달

당신은
작지만 빤짝거리며
웃어주는 별

다정히 살아온 긴 세월
오늘도 서로 마주보며
같이 나란히
지구를 내려다보며
은은한 별빛과 달빛을 내려 비추네.

STAR AND MOON

Hanging in the air
the star and the moon.

Like an affectionate couple
am I the moon? Or the star?
I am the big round moon.

You are
a small but sparkling
and smiling star.

Many years spent closely
looking at each other
side-by-side
looking down upon the earth
beaming down soft starlight and moonlight.

우리 어머니

떨어져있는 아이들이 보고 싶네.
어머니! 아버지! 하고
부르는 소리 듣고 싶네.
내가 불러 본 적이 오래된 사랑의 호칭
어머니, 아버지 실컷 듣고 싶구나.

어머니 마지막 음성을
들은 지도 어연 18년
"새벽 예배 시간이다"라고
호령치는 소리에
눈 부비며 일어나는 아침
어머니의 간곡한 기도소리.

학교에서 돌아오면
복습 숙제를 챙기시던 엄격한 어머니,
교회, 학교 가서 첫째
유행가도 화토놀이도 금지
사윗감도 예수 믿는 집안이야 되지.

성경을 줄줄 외우며
18년 간 연속 부인회 회장
부인들 놓고 호령 치던 그 유창한 응변
그 목소리 그 우아한 얼굴
이젠 꿈속에서나 들려온다.

MY MOTHER

I long for my scattered children.
Mother! Father! I want
to hear those calls.
Those affectionate titles I haven't used in a long while
Mother! Father! I want to hear earful.

Eighteen years have passed
since last I heard my mother's voice,
woken up by the
commanding voice,
"It's time for the dawn worship!"
waking up, rubbing the eyes, in the morning
with the sound of mother's earnest prayers.

After school,
my strict mother oversaw homework reviews.
At the church and school, foremostly,
the popular songs and Hwato card games were
prohibited,
and the son-in-law has to be from a Christian family.

She who could recite the Bible from memory
chaired the church women's committee
for 18 consecutive years
commanding the women with her eloquent oratory.
That voice that refined countenance
now I only hear in my dreams.

로맨스의 도시

끝없이 명상하면서
Baltic강을 달려
전설과 로맨스의 도시
코펜하겐.

넓은 바닷가에 선
작은 인어상
미지에 대한 상상을
더욱 더 촉진한다.

호기심
모험, 기대, 꿈, 포부, 희망
모두 이런 것이
우리의 삶을
값있게 장식한다.

인생은 환상으로
장식될 때
값있는
삶을 살 수 있다.

THE CITY OF ROMANCE

Endlessly contemplating
through the Baltic Sea
the city of legends and romance
Copenhagen.

By the wide sea
the Little Mermaid statue
stirs even more
the fantasy of the unknown.

The curiosity
adventures, expectations, dreams, aspirations, hopes
all these things
richly adorn
our lives.

When life is adorned
with illusions
one can live
a rich life.

당신과 걷는 이 길

인생의 마지막 길까지
당신과 같이 걸어왔습니다.
이제 당신과 같이 가는 마지막 길
아픔과 번뇌를 다 내려놓고
같이 가는 길 얼마나 기쁩니까?

달빛이 쓸고 간 이 길을
이제 이 땅의 일로
가슴 아파할 필요 없이
달빛을 맞으며 당신과 함께
걷고 있는 것 얼마나 기쁩니까?

바람도 없이 흐르는 구름에
이 세상의 모든 것 흘러 보내고
흘러 간 것 다시 돌아오지 않아도
영원한 사랑만 안고
당신과 가는 길 얼마나 기쁩니까?

THIS PATH WHERE I WALK WITH YOU

On to the last road of life,
I came walking with you to this path.
This would be the last road with you,
unburdened of pain and anguish,
how joyful is this path we share?

The road the moonlight has swept,
no longer would be with
painful heartaches of this land,
under the stream of moonlight,
how joyful is this walk with you?

Like the cloud that floats without breeze,
let us let all the pains of this land float away,
even if those that floated away never come back,
with everlasting love embraced,
how joyful it is this path where I walk with you?

친구들

그리운 친구들 또 모였구나.
흰 머리카락
주름살도
하나씩 늘었고

주름살 속에
찍힌 그들의 노고
경제 발전과 교육에
일생을 바친 그들

무거운 짐 다 내려놓고
정처 없이 흘러가는 구름처럼
한가한 인생을
누릴 수도 있지만

남은 인생을 값있게
살아보려는 미련 때문에
또 모여들은 친구들
그들은 지혜롭다.

FRIENDS

Long-missed friends gathered again.
Graying hair
wrinkles
increased one after the other

and within the wrinkles
lie the imprints of their hard work
having spent their lives
on financial security and education

having released from their burdens
like aimlessly wandering clouds
they could enjoy
idle lives

but longing to live
the rest of life for worthy causes
the friends gathered again;
they are wise.

박윤수 시인의 시세계

조 윤 호
(시인 · 해외문학 발행인)

박윤수 시인은 현실 생활에서 시의 주제를 찾고 있다. 그는 자연의 이미지를 통해 인생철학을 시에 담아낸다. 신비하게 보이기만 했던 저 달의 이미지로 그가 태어난 고향에 대한 그리움을 시로 보여줌으로써 그의 정체성을 표출해 내고 있다.

그의 대표시 가운데 「실 비치에 뜬 달」은 그가 상상력을 통해 찾아낸 객관적 상관물이다. 그는 "허공에 매달린 저 달 속에서/ 꿈과 희망과 기쁨을 찾고/ 남은 삶의 평온을 찾고자/ 아무리 밝아도 쳐다보지 않던 달/ 왜 오늘은 이렇게 보고 싶을까?"하고 읊고 있다. 이렇게 찾아낸 객관적 상관물인 달에서 그는 신을 떠올린다. 그의 시는 신이 죽은 것이 아니라 신과 함께 동행하면서 꿈과 희망과 그리고 기쁨을 찾고, 나약한 인간의 한계와 절벽을 극복해 낸다.

왜 그럴까? 시인은 그의 시 상당 부분에서 신을 신뢰하고 보이지 않는 신의 사역인 인간 봉사를 몸소 실천하여 행복을 추구하기 때문이라고 판단된다.

박윤수 시인은 뒤늦게 뛰어든 시인에 속한다. 하지만 그는 과학계에서 빛을 내고 은퇴한 후 시문학에 입문한 노 시인이다.

그는 천재적인 과학자였으나 현재는 미주문단에서 드물게 볼만큼 성공한 시인의 시세계로 보폭을 넓혔다.

THE POETIC WORLD OF THE POET PARK

by Yoon-Ho Cho

Poet Yoon Soo Park seeks his poetic subjects and themes from the reality of life. He presents the introspection of life through the imagery of nature in his poems. The ever -mysterious image of the moon evokes his longing for his hometown where he was born, expressing his identity.

Among his major works, *The Moon over the Seal Beach* shows how he found the objective correlative in his imagination. He says, "within the large moon hanging upon the space / I seek out the dreams and hopes and joy / looking for peace for my remaining days. / The moon I never looked upon, no matter how bright. / Why do I yearn to see the moon tonight?" From this found objective correlative, he brings forth God. In his poem, God is not dead. One finds dreams and hopes and joy while being side-by-side with God. And that is how we overcome the weak limits and precipice of being a human.

Why is that? We could judge from the majority of his poems he has trust in God and we see how he seeks happiness by carrying out His unseen ministry of service.

Poet Yoon Soo Park began his literary career much later in his life. He is renowned in the field of science and has debuted as a poet after his retirement. He was a genius scientist but now a rare one of poets who strides in noticeable success as a poet in the Korean-American literary scene.

127

작가에 관하여

박윤수는 1929년 경상북도 예천에서 출생, 서울대학교 문리대 물리학과를 졸업했다. 미국에 유학하여 University of Alberta 대학에서 물리학 석사, University of Cincinnati 대학원에서 물리학 박사학위를 받았다. 전북대학교 명예 이학박사이며 Rensselaer Polytechnic Institute 초빙교수와 서울대학교 초빙교수 역임, Johns Hopkins 대학교 초빙교수 역임했다. 「해외문학」 신인문학상 시부문에 당선되어 데뷔. 그는 「해외문인협회」(미국) 부회장으로 활동하고 있다.

ABOUT THE AUTHOR

Yoon Soo Park: Park was born in Yecheon, North Gyeongsang-buk-do Province. He graduated from Seoul National University. From the University of Alberta, he received a Bachelor's degree in physics and Ph.D. in physics from the University of Cincinnati. He received an honorary Ph.D. from Chonbuk National University. Park was also a visiting professor at the Rensselaer Polytechnic Institute, Seoul National University, and Johns Hopkins University. He made his literary debut by receiving the Korean Expatriate Literary "New Poet Award." He serves as Vice-President of the Korean Expatriate Literary Associaton.